Photo Credits
Cover and internals: Okhotnikova/Shutterstock

Published by Simple Truths, an imprint of Sourcebooks, Inc.
P.O. Box 4410, Naperville, Illinois 60567-4410
(630) 961-3900
Fax: (630) 961-2168
www.sourcebooks.com

Printed and bound in China.
QL 10 9 8 7 6 5 4 3 2 1

CHANGE
YOUR WORDS,
CHANGE
YOUR WORLD

A DAILY QUOTE *for Your*

EXTRAORDINARY DAY

NIDO R. QUBEIN

simple truths
small books. BIG IMPACT.

Dear Readers,

As the saying goes, "Death is inevitable. Life is short. What are you doing about it?"

What are *you* doing about it?

Are you making every day, every moment count? Are you grateful for oxygen? For friends and family? For work and leisure?

Your life is measured by who and how you influence and impact others. Purpose leads to passion, energy, action, success, and significance. Significance leads to the one result we all want—happiness.

Much of our life journey depends on our attitude, our beliefs, our behaviors, and our *words*.

This book of daily quotes includes thoughts extracted from my books, speeches, seminars, and recordings. It takes you a minute to read a page each day. That's it. But that minute could turn you in a direction loaded with serendipities worth exploring.

I believe in the art of the possible—that there is no such thing as unrealistic dreams, only unrealistic timelines. As a consultant and coach to businesses and executives around the world, I've seen lives changed through the purposeful adjustment of attitude and spirit. As president of High Point University in North Carolina, I've watched shy, reserved students transform their demeanor to one of pride and a focused future.

> **I believe in the art of the possible.**

This book is about cultivating your life as a ritual of choices—the daily choice to remain positive even when you are surrounded by negativity, to stay upbeat even when life's music may be somber, or to be grateful even when you feel like you have nothing.

When you change your words, when you transform your mindset, when you examine your beliefs, you will change your focus, and you begin to change your world.

Place this book in a visible spot in your home or office. Read a page a day, and watch the transformation begin.

Sincerely,

Nido R. Qubein

nqubein@highpoint.edu

For many people, change is more threatening than challenging. They see it as the destroyer of what is familiar and comfortable rather than the creator of what is new and exciting.

Most of us miss our best opportunities in life because they come to us disguised as hard work.

Good leaders must become
what they want their
followers to become.

The person who can laugh often and who finds humor in even the most stressful events can keep going when others are falling by the wayside. Learn to look for the humor in every situation—you'll live longer and have a lot more fun.

Your acquaintances fall into three basic categories: those who will cheer for you whether you win or lose, those who will pull for you to fail, and those who don't care one way or the other. Choose well!

Successful people don't avoid risks.
They learn to manage them.
They don't dive off cliffs into
unexplored waters; they learn
how deep the water is and
make sure there are no hidden
obstacles. Then they plunge in.

If what you are doing
is worth doing, hang in
there until it is done.

Many people deny themselves the pleasure of living life to the fullest because they follow limited visions. They dream modest dreams, so they compile modest achievements. The limiting factor is not their capacity to achieve, but their willingness to believe in themselves.

Creative people look at the future as a big adventure instead of a looming threat.

Your most frequently used tool
should be your imagination,
not your memory.

JANUARY
11

Success comes to truly
successful people as a series
of little successes rather
than as one big break.

Keep your lenses clear. Successful people perceive the world neither through pink lenses nor gray ones. They prefer clear lenses that portray the world as it is because that's the world they must deal with. If you're looking at a gray reality, don't despair. Just shift your attention to another part of the picture. There's a bright side to almost every situation. Find it, and focus on it.

What you value determines
the principles by which you
measure your behavior.

You may have the loftiest goals, the highest ideals, the noblest dreams, but remember this: nothing works unless you do.

JANUARY
15

When something becomes
personal, it becomes important.

Are you a thermometer or a thermostat? A thermometer only reflects the temperature of its environment, adjusting to the situation. But a thermostat initiates action to change the temperature in its environment.

Material success may result in
the accumulation of possessions,
but only spiritual success will
enable you to enjoy them.

Putting things off has seldom been associated with winning. It's the losers who wait for things to happen. The winners in the game of life *make* things happen.

It is important to measure your performance against your past success, but it is even more important to measure your performance against your potential.

You won't know if you're moving toward your goals unless you have some way of measuring the motion.

Training teaches people to follow prescriptions. Education teaches people to make choices.

The only way to keep from making mistakes is to do nothing—and that's the biggest mistake of all.

When your life is possession-centered, the important thing is what you have; when it is principle-centered, the important thing is who and what you are.

Make a strong, permanent commitment to invest your talents only in pursuits that deserve your best efforts.

Success is not an either/or proposition: either work or pleasure, either the party or the grindstone. Success consists of finding a happy balance between work and pleasure. In fact, truly successful people make their work a part of their pleasure.

Objections are the salesperson's most valuable source of feedback.

Losers do what is required of them, or even less, but winners always do more than is required— and they do it with enthusiasm.

The way most of us procrastinate is to do nothing about anything we should be doing something about.

Success doesn't come to you;
you must go to it. The trail
is well-traveled. If you want
to walk it, you can.

When a goal matters enough
to a person, that person will
find a way to accomplish what
at first seemed impossible.

People don't respond to what you say; they respond to what they understand you to say.

Only when your memories
are more important than
your goals are you old.

No one ever becomes perfect,
but anyone can improve.

Listen twice as much as you
talk. Others will hear twice
as much of what you say.

Goals help you keep what's really important in perspective, so you don't spend all of your time doing what seems urgent.

When you find yourself on a
plateau, look for another level.

Many people are unable to prepare
for the future because they're
too busy rehearsing the past.

Professionals are willing to take intelligent risks, accepting the possibility of failure as a fair price for the opportunity to grow.

Those who spend their lives searching for happiness never find it, while those who search for meaning, purpose, and strong personal relationships find that happiness usually comes to them as a by-product of those three things.

Whatever keeps you from reaching your goals today had better be important. It's costing you a day of your life!

The difference between mediocrity and excellence lies in inner qualities and not external skills.

If you could view your life as you do a highway from an airliner, many of the detours and curves would make more sense.

Seek to know others.
You'll be amazed at how it will
help you understand yourself.

Knowledge is to creativity what
a bed of coals is to a fire: it
provides a reservoir of resources
to keep the creative fires burning.
To develop creativity, acquire
a thirst for knowledge.

Only when you love and
are loved can you reach your full
potential as a human being.
Happy Valentine's Day!

Don't waste your time worrying about insignificant things; instead, focus your time on what you can achieve.

We're inclined to excuse in ourselves behavior that we find unacceptable in others.

Let's not make excuses; we should hold ourselves to the very same standards, if not higher, than we hold our peers.

High-powered communicators focus words the way laser beams focus light.

The interesting thing about procrastination is that it has more to do with what we fail to do than with what we do.

Most people tend to remember more about the feeling a speech creates than they do about the content of the message it delivers.

FEBRUARY 21

Focus on your audience
and creating an emotional
connection with them.

Goals are simply a way
of breaking a vision into
smaller, workable units.

Each of us has the freedom to choose how we will respond to the circumstances in which we find ourselves.

Choose to have a positive outlook on life. You'll notice a measurable difference in your mood and overall happiness.

Competence leads to confidence.

Learn as much as you can, prepare yourself, and practice, practice, practice! The rewards will follow.

Greet every person you meet cheerfully and enthusiastically. Nobody can fake cheerfulness and enthusiasm very long. You'll either quit trying or improve your outlook.

Winners compare their achievements with their goals, while losers compare their achievements with those of other people.

Achieving your vision doesn't mean you've reached the end of the line; it simply means that you've come to a new starting place.

Self-centered people tend to monopolize the talking; secure people tend to monopolize the listening.

Losers blame their circumstances; winners rise above their circumstances. Which attitude will you take?

Love is the most positive force
on earth, and each of us
can cultivate it.

Behavior that goes consistently
unrewarded will eventually
be discontinued.

What matters is not so much
how you got to be the way you
are now, but what you do with
the person you have become.

Whether you are a success or a failure in life has little to do with your circumstances; it has much more to do with your choices!

Losers ask "Can I do it?" Winners ask "How can I do it?" Losers are guided by what's impossible. Winners are guided by what's possible.

An extraordinary person is someone who consistently does the things ordinary people can't or won't do.

What you are and hope to be is the way you experience yourself, but other people experience you by what you do. Watch your actions, and strive to live up to your ideal self.

Procrastination is a thief
that robs you of money by
stealing your time.

If you believe you can, and believe it strongly enough, you will be amazed at what you can do.

Don't mistake the difficult
for the impossible.

Your present circumstances
don't determine where you
can go; they merely determine
where you start.

People who invariably put themselves first will find that others tend to put them last.

Success rarely comes to those
who are expecting failure.

The key to scheduling your time
is to focus on objectives,
not on activities.

Many potential innovators failed to dream, and many dreamers failed to make their dreams become reality.

Nobody likes to be around a person who is always looking at the dark side of life.

Admire your heroes.
Adapt from your models.
Learn from your mentors.

MARCH
20

Being genuinely helpful to other
people not only makes you
feel better about yourself—it
is also good business.

Change brings opportunity.

Hatred is the most destructive force on earth. It does the most damage to those who harbor it.

To be a great person, walk
hand in hand and side by
side with great people.

Learn to be gracious—
whether you win or lose.

Disguising incompetence
doesn't alter the basic condition.

Up close, the earth looks flat.
From outer space, it's round. The
difference is in perspective.

Successful, self-starting individuals seek responsibility. They take calculated risks and don't make excuses to cover up their inactivity.

People worry for only two reasons. Either they stand to lose something they want to keep, or they stand not to gain something they want to get. If keeping something you have costs you your peace of mind, or if something you stand to gain takes you to the brink of distress, it makes sense to ask yourself whether what you are worried over is worth the price.

What if you could be anything, or
anybody, you chose to be?
Think about it!
What would you choose to be?

A decision is made with the brain. A commitment is made with the heart. Therefore, a commitment is much deeper and more binding than a decision.

Enthusiastic people experience
life from the inside out.

APRIL
1

Nonperformers focus on obstacles;
performers focus on results.

The leader who can't communicate can't create the conditions that motivate.

What you choose is what you get. You cannot whine to the world about where you are in life, because the truth is, you made choices in your life that somehow directly or indirectly got you to where you are. Most of the time, we can control much of our destiny by our attitudes and by our actions.

A habit is nothing but an action
that has become automatic.

Wherever you are, whatever your circumstances may be, whatever misfortune you may have suffered, the music of your life has not gone. It's inside you—if you listen to it, you can hear it.

The organization that can't communicate can't change, and the corporation that can't change is dead.

If what you're working for really matters, you'll give it all you've got.

Don't interrupt, but
be interruptible.

Make education a continuing,
never-ending process.

When we dread doing something, it's usually easier—for the moment—to come up with an excuse. Unfortunately, most of us find dread to be counterproductive, because the longer we dread the task, the worse it seems.

To live, you must
have a purpose to guide you.

Fixing the blame is never important,
and fixing the relationship
is never unimportant.

People stay in ruts because it takes less effort to follow the rut than to get out of it.

The process of growing and
learning always involves risk.

What you say does not
have nearly the impact as
the way you say it.

Do you manage your time, or
does your time manage you?

Applying your talents without reference to your values and principles is like using your car's accelerator without touching the steering wheel.

If you do your best only when you feel like doing your best, your work will probably be pretty shabby.

Enthusiasm is the light of creativity and insight.

People who are poor listeners will find few who are willing to come to them with useful information.

Set goals that are consistent
with your purpose in life.

Make a strong commitment
to reach your full potential
as a human being.

Training is anchored to
the past. Education looks
toward the future.

Throughout life, be sure to accumulate good memories.

Human beings have both an overwhelming capacity to love and an overriding need to love and be loved.

When you think "Why won't somebody do something about this?" try to remember that you are somebody.

Do your tasks.

Achieve your goals.

Live with purpose.

Teaching skills to people without giving them a vision for a better future—a vision based on common values—is only training.

May the future you create
exceed your fondest
expectations!

It's okay to be disappointed;
it's never okay to be discouraged.
See the difference, and
strive to never give up.

MAY

1

The power of commitment comes from within you. It's there, and you may not even know it.

Many people looking for meaning in their lives find it by losing themselves in causes greater than they are.

Accept each moment as a gift
to be received with joy.

The good moments of the present
are the good memories you
will carry into your future.

When we see things in
perspective, we see them in
their proper relationships as
to value or importance.

There's so much
to see, to do, to be! Life is full
of choices. Choose wisely.

You can live every day of your life.
You can be alive to the tips of
your fingers. You can accomplish
virtually any worthwhile goal
you set for yourself.

No mistake you could ever make will strip you of your value as a human being. Most mistakes detour you only slightly on your road to fulfilling your purpose.

Learn to be kind to yourself. Keep a list of your triumphs and successes. As you focus on what you have done, you will have more confidence in what you can do.

Goal setting illuminates the road to success just as runway lights illuminate the landing field for an incoming aircraft.

The past is over. Enjoy the good memories, learn from the bad ones, and get ready to make some new ones. Your focus should be on the future.

Gratitude does not come easily for most people, because focusing our attention on what we want or need is easier than acknowledging what we have received. If you want to build and maintain a healthy balance in your relationship with yourself and others, develop an active sense of gratitude.

With lifelong education,
learning becomes a
renewable resource.

While some only do what is required of them, achievers always endeavor to go beyond the required and into the extraordinary. And what's more—they do so with enthusiasm.

Spiritual values transcend the material artifacts that we can touch and see. They take us into the realm of beauty, inspiration, and love.

Success is an empty attainment
if it doesn't bring happiness.

A "monologue in duet" happens when I think about what I'm going to say while you're saying what you thought about while I was talking.

To acquire balance means to achieve that happy medium between the minimum and the maximum that represents your optimum. The minimum is the least you can get by with. The maximum is the most you're capable of. The optimum is the amount or degree of anything that is most favorable toward the ends you desire.

When you identify something that you do well, that you enjoy doing, and that supports the values that are important to you, you have defined success in your terms.

When you can see the humor
in embarrassing situations,
they cease to be stressful.

The power comes from
within you. It's there, and you
may not even know it.

Cultivate a sense of humor.
Humor is the pleasant
lubricant of life.

Conquer the anxiety habit, and you can reduce your chances of distress. Don't worry about it—do it!

Some people procrastinate so much that all they can do is run around like firefighters all day, putting out fires that should not have gotten started in the first place.

In choosing your purpose in life, you have to answer three big questions: Who am I? What am I doing here? Where am I going?

Acquire a learning mentality.

The trouble with many plans is that they are based on the way things are now. To be successful, your personal plan must focus on what you want, not what you have.

Cultivate love
by banishing hatred.

Learn to accept constructive criticism and to ignore petty criticism.

The key to emotional health is to learn how to handle grief. The person who reacts to sorrow only with anger becomes embittered, hardened, and cynical.

If a task is worth doing, it is worth doing at the earliest reasonable time. If it is not worth doing, forget it!

People can be unreliable and disloyal;
possessions can lose their value;
jobs that once stimulated you
can become boring—but principles
remain steady through it all.

Above all, be true to yourself, and
as surely as day follows night,
you can't be false to anyone.

Make it a habit to say nice things about yourself to yourself. You'll find that you like yourself better.

Unconscious choices put you at the mercy of the dice roll.

Your successes and failures are never due to circumstance but rather entirely due to your attitude. Your mindset, your choices, and your faithful courage will make up your achievement in life.

Value people, not things. People who are happy and successful learn to value people and to use things. People who are looking for something to make them happy somehow never find it. Yet those who find a way to be happy while they are looking for something good benefit in two ways: not only are they usually happy while they are looking, but they also typically find what they are looking for.

Nothing softens the blows of life
like a good sense of humor.

Training teaches how.
Education teaches why.

Some concentrate on the blank wall that boxes them in; winners always look for a way to get under it, over it, around it, or through it.

Good habits are hard to develop,
but they are easy to live with.
Bad habits are easy to develop,
but they are hard to live with.
Develop good habits.

Success is mainly a question of attitude. If you go into an undertaking expecting to succeed, the odds are great that you'll succeed. If you go in fearful of losing, you're more likely to lose. Cultivate a winning attitude. It will sustain you even when the odds seem stacked against you.

You can let the future happen, or you can create it. You create it by forming a clear, vivid picture of what you want and fixing your mental and emotional eyes on that picture. Let it become your vision, and it will draw you toward fulfillment.

Make it a habit to go about
every day looking for things you
can change for the better.

Attitude makes all the difference. With a good attitude, you don't dwell on the bad aspects of your life. You allow yourself to enjoy the good times. With a bad attitude, you waste good moments worrying about the past or dreading the future.

Cultivate the art of looking at events in their proper relationship to your whole life. Often, something appears for the moment to be a tragedy, but it becomes only a minor annoyance when taken in the context of your total life.

It isn't enough to act friendly—you have to be friendly. That means you have to cultivate a genuinely positive attitude and a genuine concern for others.

Optimist or pessimist? It's your choice. Whether you are an optimist or a pessimist, the choice of how you will be in the future is yours, and yours alone. If you are like the people who aren't happy unless they are miserable, you can stay that way. If you want to be joyful, enthusiastic, and excited about life, you can be, regardless of your circumstances.

A vision bypasses circumstances. It finds a way around them, over them, or under them. Or it rearranges the circumstances. One way or another, it will take you toward your objectives.

A change of attitude is like changing your mind; you just decide you are going to change the way you see things. You can't just pretend you have a good attitude; you have to have a good attitude. You have to look at the bright side of the situations, the good side of people—including yourself—and the positive side of negative events.

If you want to reach for success in every area of your life, the most important asset you can have is a faithfully optimistic, winning attitude.

You can't take charge of your life without an awareness of where you've been, where you are, and where you are going. But you can't build your life on the past. The past is gone. Nor can you allow your destiny to be limited by present circumstances. The present is fleeting. The only place left to build your life is in the future.

Don't seek improvement;
seek excellence.

To make motivation pay off, you have to mobilize all of your resources in the direction of your goals. Mobilizing yourself involves deciding what you want, then determining what will get you what you want.

If you don't like the way
things are, complaining won't
change them. Action will.

You are the product of your choices. We can't grow by repeatedly following prescriptions. We can grow only by making new choices. We are the sum total of the choices we have made in the past. We can change what we are in the future through the choices we make today. Choose well.

Most of the limitations that keep us from realizing our full potential are artificial. They are imposed on us by circumstances or by other people.

Remember that the cards you're dealt are less important than the way you play your hand. Circumstances may be beyond your control, but you have full control of your responses.

Although maturity involves many things, it certainly includes taking charge of our lives through a series of rational decisions—rather than allowing our emotions to rule us.

Of all the human abilities, love is the most noble. It is by far the most powerful force in the universe. Love moves the spirit to create, the mind to think, and the body to perform.

Life should be an adventure, to be savored from beginning to end. It is a game of constantly changing odds, constantly developing challenges, constantly opening opportunities. To win it, you have to play it. Sitting on the sidelines won't do. Even after you've achieved all you ever hoped to achieve, it's no time to stop living.

JULY

1

The quickest way to cast out negative thoughts is to feed enough positive thoughts into your mind that there is no longer room for the negative ones.

Put good stress into your life. A person who is experiencing no stress is also experiencing no challenge, and people who are not challenged will not exert themselves to succeed.

Winners are proactive, not reactive. They create new circumstances rather than simply responding to them. Reactive people are likely to go through life complaining about their circumstances. They focus on things they can do nothing about and ignore the things that are within their circle of influence. Proactive people look for ways to succeed in spite of any circumstances.

Life is a smorgasbord of choices. Yet here we stand, with our small plates that can hold only so much. Freedom demands that we make choices.

Take a positive view of mistakes. If you goof royally, don't beat yourself up. Congratulate yourself on the lesson you learned.

You can maximize your chances of success by assessing, categorizing, and prioritizing your challenges. Ignore those challenges that are unlikely to affect your success and happiness either way. Look for ways to adjust to those situations that you can do nothing about. Focus your efforts on the things you can change.

Know the difference between productive failures and nonproductive successes.

Surround yourself with positive influences. When you are surrounded by negative thinkers, images, or materials, it is easy to get bogged down in hopelessness.

The human mind, coupled with an indomitable spirit and a miraculous physical body, is capable of creating in a way that is unknown anywhere else in the universe. Even when a physical body is limited in certain key areas, the human mind and spirit can break free to create in the most amazing ways.

Success in almost any undertaking requires that you engage in risk taking, and with each risk comes the element of fear. How you respond to the fear makes the difference between success and failure.

A positive attitude is like love in at least one respect: the more you give, the more you get.

Learn to hold your mistakes and failures in proper perspective. You can build and maintain your self-confidence by balancing your failures and mistakes against your long-term goals, your underlying purpose in life, and your inherent worth as a human being rather than against their immediate consequences.

The person who finishes another's sentences, denies another's right to a differing opinion, and approaches others with suspicion is destined to spend a great deal of time alone.

Some things within your circle of concern are beyond your control. Concentrate on the things you can do something about.

What's past is past; what's done is done. The important thing is what you can do now to achieve the future you want. This requires a willingness not only to accept change, but also to pursue it proactively.

JULY
16

All meaningful change
comes from within.

Each of us can, and does, control how we react to what others do to us, how we cope with what happens to us, how well we use the physical abilities we have, what we do with the resources we have been given, how we respond to the opinions of others, and whether we can, or will, live up to others' expectations.

Our emotions are our least dependable, and often our most deceptive, sensing devices. Be sure to master your feelings; don't let them master you.

People value authenticity,
even ahead of charisma.

If you want the kind of happiness and deep personal satisfaction out of life that circumstances cannot destroy, search until you find what you can do best, what no one could pay you money not to do, what you would gladly pay for the privilege of doing. Then do it with all that is within you. Your passion will lead you to success and significance.

If you want a formula for becoming miserable, the first rule is to think only of yourself. People who think only of themselves, and what they want, find it hard to be happy with anything they get.

People who enjoy mental and emotional balance are self-reliant and self-determining. They don't blame their troubles or shortcomings on any person, circumstance, or system.

If you create tension, you get resistance. If you create trust, you get response.

To seize the day, you have to make an irrevocable commitment to act. You do this by wiping the slate clean, creating a new script, and embarking on a course from which there is no turning back.

Total, unconditional acceptance of yourself is the first step in building a positive self-image.

Some people see themselves as doing a job. Winners see themselves as part of all humankind and their work as their contribution to a better world.

Physical barriers and disabilities are not the real limitations that rob us of our freedom to make the best of what we have and of what we are. The real limitations have to do with the way we see ourselves and the world around us. Our attitudes hold us back from becoming all that we were created to be.

When you accept yourself totally,
you are free to accept other people.

JULY
29

When you're sizing up your capacities, allow for the "and then some." The "and then some" provides you with positive stress that enables you to meet the challenge—and then some.

Many people are not willing to pay the price to be successful. Maybe that's why so many withdraw into their comfort zones. They long for a place to rest, a place to be safe, a place to be comforted and coddled.

Those who are afraid to fail
may not deserve to succeed.

People who have strong self-confidence tend to

apply their personal power to useful goals.

They let others talk about their abilities and deeds.

They concentrate on goals, not activities. And they

freely express admiration and appreciation to others.

AUGUST

2

Commitment involves feelings as
well as thinking. It is the result
of a well-documented formula:
thoughts + feelings = action.

220 | NIDO R. QUBEIN

People with bad attitudes have a hard time finding people who don't have something wrong with them. And when they do find someone they can tolerate, they often chase them away with negative thoughts and feelings.

Information without wisdom
gets us nowhere.

Listening is to hearing what speaking is to talking. Hearing is the natural response of your ears to sound. But listening is using your ears and your mind to absorb and understand what the other person is saying.

People who have positive self-esteem tend to be genuinely helpful to other people. In fact, the two tendencies go together so well that it is hard to tell which produces the other.

Make it a point to read or watch or listen to something positive and inspiring at least once every day.

AUGUST
8

People with a winner's attitude know that fame and fortune are not the only measures of success. Public recognition and money are only superficial ways of keeping score. What drives the winners to put forth Herculean effort, to bounce back from failures and defeats, to overcome handicaps, to battle discouragement and fear is the knowledge that they are involved in a purpose that is bigger than they are.

Style attracts.

Substance retains.

Taking the positive view requires more than simply casting out negative thoughts, although that is an important part of it. Positive input must replace negative thoughts.

Challenged people are excited and ready for action. They're like a talented, well-trained team going into a championship game. The challenge of winning fills the team members with an exciting tension that puts the edge on their performance, causing them to play at their best—and win.

Charisma gets you
in the door, but it takes
substance to deliver results.

Most of us tend to suffer from "agenda anxiety," the feeling that what we want to say to others is more important than what we think they might want to say to us.

Have confidence in yourself. Self-confidence is often little more than a feeling, way down in the pit of your stomach, that you can do something that seems impossible. But as you respond positively to that little feeling, it grows and grows until it reaches full bloom in concrete action.

The standard to aim for is excellence, not improvement.

Without wisdom, we are unlikely to take the measured steps required to build a satisfying future. We are unlikely to distinguish between sound counsel and faulty advice.

Mistakes are seldom fatal. It's your attitude toward mistakes that can cost you. Those who can come out of each mistake or failure better equipped to face the future are able to not only salvage self-confidence, but also to build it even stronger.

Excellence is a quality
of heart and soul, not of
mechanical processes.

Exercising wisdom does not require super intellect; geniuses can act foolishly, and people of ordinary intelligence can act wisely.

Comfort zones are like caves: their darkness makes it hard to see. Their stagnant air grows stale and becomes hard to breathe. Their walls box us in. Their low ceilings keep us from stretching to our full height. Dare to venture outside of your comfort zone.

Happiness is to fulfillment
what Internet chat rooms are
to human conversation.

When we apply information and knowledge with wisdom, our words and actions influence others. We become persons of substance.

Wisdom does not require encyclopedic knowledge. A head full of information is like a dictionary full of words: just as the words in a dictionary can produce great literature or incoherent babble, the information in our heads may produce wise or irresponsible decisions.

Wisdom does not come
from constant success; it
comes from lessons learned
through repeated failures.

Happiness is a thing of the moment. Fulfillment is lasting.

Time management makes each minute count. Life management makes your whole existence count.

Acquire wisdom, and treat it as the valuable asset it is. If all you have is information, people will use you and then discard you. If all you have is knowledge, people will need you until such a time as their own level of knowledge is equal to yours or in their view is sufficient. But if you have wisdom, people will respect you.

You must view your life as being in a constant state of improvement. Plan your actions purposely to improve what is already there.

Excellence is the quality that distinguishes the extraordinary from the ordinary.

Minimize urgent tasks by spotting problems while they're still minor and easily remedied and take care of them at once. If you keep in perspective what's really important, you won't spend all your time doing what seems urgent.

Return on investment is a way to measure profit. Return on life is a way to measure significant impact and fulfillment.

Fun is momentary.

Joy is everlasting.

Fulfillment is enduring.

When we invest our lives in responding to urgencies, we allow circumstances and other people to choose how we will live. If we don't have a clearly defined, focused objective to work on at any given moment, we're likely to spend our lives putting out brush fires.

You can acquire the habit of excellence by cultivating your teachability, adaptability, flexibility, creativity, and sensitivity.

To be authentic, you must consciously
and intentionally bring your business,
social, spiritual, and family lives
into such harmony that a person
looking at your performance
in these roles will know what
kind of person you really are.

Balanced people are other-oriented, constantly looking for ways to improve the world they live in and for ways to attract the support of people who will help them.

Ordinary performers wait until they need help to seek advice. Extraordinary performers cultivate friendships with the experts before they need the expertise. Then, when they need help, it's readily available.

When you're balanced, you don't wait for opportunities to serve your fellow humans. You look for them.

Income is temporary;

value is permanent.

Cultivate a love for learning and a capacity for earning. These qualities are important ingredients for life.

Your legacy depends on what
you choose to put at the center
of your life. You can make riches
and fame your twin goals. Or you
can choose to make this planet a
better place for everything on it.

SEPTEMBER
11

The things people really are
passionate about are those that come
directly from their sense of service.

Success is focused on tasks, even goals. Significance focuses on purpose. When you set your sights on living a life of significance, you use your talents to make this world a better place and work to plant seeds of greatness in the lives of those around you.

When we associate with leaders, we tend to aim high, because our associates aim high. We need the company of the best to stretch us toward higher achievement.

The most gratifying reward comes when we give not because we have to, not because someone asks us to, not because we owe it, but rather out of hearts filled with gratitude.

SEPTEMBER 15

Sustainable confidence
comes from competence and
leads to commitment.

People whose hearts are full of gratitude tend to be more positive, generous, and innovative. They also tend to be easier to get along with—and, therefore, are more successful and influential.

Self-interest is a wonderful thing, but enlightened self-interest is ten times better. It's not about what we get; it's really about what we give.

Nobody likes to work around self-centered people. People who see themselves at the center of the universe often believe that everyone else thinks the way they do. This can lead them to think that their way of thinking is the only valid way of thinking. Such an attitude closes the door to a lot of constructive and creative ideas.

A legacy is what you bequeath to humanity. If it's a good legacy, its benefits will remain long after your name has been forgotten.

Success does not guarantee joy.
To turn success into joy, add
significance and fulfillment.

Good stress can be used like the tension in a bowstring. Unless you stress the bow and the string, your arrow won't fly straight to its mark. Good stress is fruitful friction—it allows you to produce the results that you're aiming for.

The strength of a positive attitude comes from spreading it around.

If you want to have a great life,
enough people must say that
they need you in their lives. Be
authentic. Be someone other people
trust, and use the opportunity
to interpret your own value.

Success focuses on three *F*s:
fans, fame, fortune. Significance
also focuses on three *F*s:
faith, family, friends.

The power to affect your
future lies within your
own mind and heart.

Here's a risk management tool for every decision that has inherent risk: What's the best thing that can happen as the result of taking this risk? What's the most likely thing to happen as a result of taking this risk? What's the worst thing that can happen as a result of taking this risk?

Only love can make your success worthwhile.

No one is responsible for your success or your joy. You must search for it and be in a continual state of earning it.

The choice as to how
you will be in the future is
yours and yours alone.

To merely succeed is not an end in itself. You must use your success to impact other people and the world.

A short adjective for people who try to be who they aren't is "phony." Nobody likes a phony. Be yourself, but be your best self.

If you would reach your full potential, cultivate all of the creative urges within you, and respond to the sensitivity that cries out for expression. Develop your best and most useful skills to their maximum level.

Anxiety is the currency
of the insecure.

What the wise old masters have told us in a thousand ways boils down to this: it is easier to act your way into feeling the way you want to feel than it is to feel your way into acting the way you want to act.

Simmering resentment
saps energy.

Without a glowing vision, you'll regard your desirable future as unattainable, and you won't focus your efforts on attaining it. You will be imprisoned by your circumstances.

Some people lead their lives one task at a time without meditating on where the series of tasks is taking them. Some live at the goal level, aiming toward short-term objectives without thinking of the big picture. But the happiest people are those who live their lives at the purpose level.

If you simply wear friendliness as a mask, the first stressful situation will unmask you, and people will spot you for a phony.

Courtesy is the oil that
lubricates the machinery
of communication.

The word *success* does not contain an *I*. The first vowel is *U*, and until we learn to think of you instead of I, our batting average in communication and in human relations will be close to zero.

Say what you mean, precisely
what you mean, and only
what you mean.

Those who feel good about themselves long to help others feel good about themselves. The more they reach out to help others, the better they feel about themselves. Only the insecure, the frightened, those with low self-esteem approach life with an attitude that says "It's every person for himself or herself." Sadly, they find only more insecurity and lower self-esteem.

Enthusiasm is a positive inner force that makes things happen, a gracious and polite bid for attention, a method of diplomacy and persuasion, a cooperative spirit, an excitement for life.

The past can be a wonderful place to visit, but you wouldn't want to live there.

OCTOBER
15

The key to your success is to be sensitive enough to understand what other people want and generous enough to help them get it.

Those who sow abundantly
reap abundantly.

The situations you encounter in life generally fall into three categories: those you can influence, those you'd like to influence, and those that are not worth influencing.

To get where you need to be five years from now, what should you accomplish in the next year? To reach that one-year goal, what should you do in the next six months? The next month? The next week? Today?

The surest route to success today is to find out what others want and look for ways to provide it.

Success is not a matter of
luck, an accident of birth,
or a reward for virtue.

Look for and develop your "differential advantage." Your differential advantage is something you can do better than anybody else to meet the needs of the people around you. Whatever it is, find it and exploit it. Your differential advantage is your ticket to excellence.

In an age in which most things that glitter are plastic, seek to find some nuggets of gold. Treasure them.

Forget your ability to think faster than another person talks—everybody has it, but only the foolish use it.

A commitment is like your signature on a contract: it binds you to a course of action.

Talking when nobody is listening is as futile as trying to cut paper with half a pair of scissors.

Improvement is to excellence as grape juice is to champagne—it's good, but not considered the best. When you want to toast success, you don't often aim for grape juice; you aim for the bubbly. Whatever your endeavor is, make excellence the standard by which you judge your performance.

If you practice the principle of love, you will soon find your feelings taking their cue from your actions.

Integrity breeds high
self-esteem—and it earns you
a lot of friends as well.

Procrastination is delaying
anything you need or want to
do until later—when there is
no valid reason to do so.

Your beliefs lead to your behaviors,
and behaviors lead to results.
If you don't like the results,
don't fuss about your behaviors;
examine and realign your beliefs.

You're wasting your time when you try to answer questions people are not asking.

NOVEMBER
1

The time is now.

The person is you.

Nothing gets accomplished "sooner or later." It gets accomplished at a specific time and in a specific place.

When we perceive the way
things are as the way things ought
to be, our lives are in harmony.

Rarely do people move from mediocrity to excellence in one giant step. They get there by taking numerous small steps. That's improvement. But the small improvements you make day by day can accumulate like compound interest. Eventually, they'll add up to excellence.

People who put career first may end up with gold-plated résumés and rusted-out family lives.

Success can be defined in one word: *balance*. We become successful when we have achieved spiritual, familial, mental, physical, social, and economic balance.

If you work only on days
you feel like working, you'll
never amount to much.

Truly successful people know that there's something more important than ROI, or return on investment—it's ROL, return on life. ROI is what we get back from investing money; ROL is what we get back from investing ourselves.

Your best bet for a good job
is to do the best you can with
the one you have right now.

Be open to new ideas and new ways of doing things. Be willing to listen, observe, and learn constantly.

Wisdom is information
sharpened into a useful tool.

NOVEMBER

12

Goals are the intermediate
steps on the way to a vision,
mileposts on the way to success,
significance, and fulfillment. To
achieve our objectives, we must
develop action plans—step-by-step
procedures for reaching our goals.

Our value to humanity depends on how much of ourselves we give to make the world a better place.

If you take risk out of life, you take opportunity out of life.

You don't have to be a superhero to achieve excellence. All you need is a commitment to do more than ordinary people do—and do it consistently, in spite of the bumps in the road. Make that commitment today, and follow it to your promising future.

Success, significance, and achievement don't depend on what we do; they depend on who we are.

Every improvement in life is
the result of change.

The quest for excellence is an inward one. You won't find it in a book, in a seminar, or in an expensive piece of high-tech equipment. You'll find it within yourself.

True generosity involves giving, not just giving back. It means giving with no expectation of repayment.

Your life needs an outline, systems, and structures that will enable you to discipline yourself to move toward the fulfillment of your vision.

Enthusiasm is the color of inspiration and courage.

**NOVEMBER
22**

There are no unrealistic dreams,
just unrealistic timelines.

Manage your life, not just your time. Time management means knowing where you want to be at the end of the day and taking orderly steps to get there. Life management means deciding what you want on your tombstone and taking steps to make sure you earn the epitaph. Energy management ensures your battery doesn't run out before you accomplish your goals.

Be grateful.
And remember: whining is the
opposite of thanksgiving.

Big things consist of many little things—and you have to achieve the little things first.

When you create a vision for the future, don't limit yourself to the things you think are achievable, given your present circumstances.

Vision is a thing of the heart.
It's the desire that provides the
energy and the will to keep going.

Focus on activities that contribute
to the greatest value in your
life, and do more of those.

The value of taking the long view
of life is that it enables you to
see problems as opportunities,
passing up the fun-for-the-moment
to pursue a worthwhile goal.

When your efforts result in failure, look for something you can learn from the situation that will later help you accomplish what you set out to accomplish.

DECEMBER
1

We pick up habits from the crowd we associate with. So whatever it is you do, seek out the people who do it best. Observe the people who excel at their jobs. Ask for their advice, and follow their examples.

The choices you make determine
the person you become.

Fulfillment comes from a life well-lived—a life devoted to making the world a better place. When you make the world a better place to live, you become a better person.

Stop following emotional whims.
Decide what you want, decide
what you must do to obtain it,
then act on your decision.

Learn to look for humor in every situation. You'll live longer and have a lot more fun.

Try new things, building on
your successes and learning
from your mistakes.

A truly balanced person keeps expanding intellectually, interacts effectively with other people, seeks constant spiritual growth, cultivates physical fitness, maintains a healthy family environment, and guarantees economic well-being.

Don't act like the person
you need to be; become the
person you need to be.

DECEMBER
9

One rule of thumb holds that when you've done something the same way for at least two years, there's probably a better way of doing it.

Motivation without mobilization
causes frustration.

Life management means being
purposeful in the way you invest
your time, use your energy,
and spend your money.

Associate with positive people. Look for friends who feel good about themselves, people who have the attitude of gratitude. People who need to tear down others are not happy with themselves and are not good for you or your attitude.

Don't waste energy on things
that don't matter or over
which you have no control.

Isn't it ironic that some people protect their money and possessions with their lives, yet let their energy and time slip away with little thought? They don't seem to realize that time is their most valuable possession—the only part of their inventory that can never be replaced.

When you like yourself,
you will gravitate toward
people who like you.

Brevity is the very heart
of a good speech.

The genius who can't communicate
is intellectually impotent.

The truly generous don't give
back; they just give.

As adults, we need to balance five kinds of capital: financial, educational, reputational, relational, and physical.

Look for people who have their knowledge in order—business people and industrialists, community leaders, and philanthropists—from whom you can learn all kinds of principles for insightful living.

The pessimist has screened out all the exciting gifts that the present moment promises to bring, while the optimist is ready and eager to receive those gifts.

In the marketplace of life, the seller may set the price, but it is always the buyer who determines the value.

Only by learning from the mistakes of those who were successful, as well as making mistakes of your own, can you yourself find success.

People who take the positive view basically see the world as a good place. They actively look for the good in other people and situations, and they act with hope and faith.

Only by loving and supporting our fellow man can mankind achieve greatness. Therefore, only by showing love yourself can you achieve your own full potential.

A good story is to a speech
what a window is to a house—
it lets in the light.

People with adult bodies and
minds who are still ruled by
their emotions can never find
enough fun and entertainment
to satisfy their cravings.

Objections are to the salesperson what symptoms are to the medical doctor; they point to a problem that must be dealt with.

High morale can't flourish in a workplace full of conflict.

In life, you must become a "value interpreter," because in the absence of a value interpreter, everything is reduced in price.

Here's a good formula for achieving balance in life: Invest a third of your life in earning; you must have resources if you want to be able to give resources. Invest a third of your life in learning; read books and periodicals every week. Invest one third of your life in giving and service.

ABOUT THE AUTHOR

Knowing little English and having only fifty dollars in his pocket, Nido R. Qubein arrived in North Carolina with his mom's advice ringing in his ears: your education will be your ticket to your life's purpose.

He was seventeen, the youngest of five, and seven thousand miles from home. He studied hard, worked hard, and prayed. And he persevered.

Today, Dr. Qubein is one of the country's influential leaders. He is an educator, a philanthropist, an in-demand speaker, a bestselling author, a consultant, and a successful businessman with contacts worldwide.

He has been honored with many awards that include the

Ellis Island Award and Horatio Alger Award for Distinguished Americans. He also has received honorary doctorate degrees from each of his three alma maters.

He has built more than half a dozen businesses, and he has written seventeen books on leadership, business, and personal growth. Meanwhile, he and his family and friends have started a foundation that has helped hundreds of students attend college.

He has received the Cavett Award, the Oscar of professional speaking. He is a member of the Speakers Hall of Fame and Beta Gamma Sigma, the global honor society for business leaders.

Over his four-decade career as a leadership consultant, he has addressed millions of people worldwide and recorded hundreds of CDs and DVDs.

In 2005, his life's path changed. He became the seventh president of his alma mater, High Point University. Since then, he has helped lead the university through an extraordinary transformation in which $1.5 billion has been invested in the school.

HPU has expanded from 91 to 420 acres. It has added four academic schools, added more than sixty new buildings, and tripled its enrollment and faculty to 4,600 students and 300 faculty members.

From that growth has come success. For the fourth year in a row, *U.S.News & World Report* named HPU No. 1 Regional College in the South. In 2016, the magazine also ranked HPU No. 1 as the Most Innovative College in the South.

Dr. Qubein currently serves on the executive board of La-Z-Boy Inc., one of the world's largest and most recognized furniture retailers; BB&T, a Fortune 500 financial corporation; and the National Leadership Council for the Museum of the American Revolution.

This distinction complements his DAR Americanism Medal,